The One Called BOSS:
Top Keys For Effective Leadership.

TIM BRADLEY

© Copyright

INTRODUCTION

Have you ever worked with a leader who wasn't very effective? Do you know that poor leadership comes at a cost? Working with an ineffective leader can be demotivating or demoralizing, which may hamper your productivity and ability to reach your goals. This, in turn, can adversely impact business results.

Effective leadership, on the other hand, results in increased employee happiness, engagement, and retention rates. But that's not all. An engaged workforce leads to 17% higher productivity, a 10% increase in customer ratings, a 20% increase in sales, and 21% greater profitability. While few would argue with the importance of effective leadership, it can often seem like an elusive idea.
What is effective leadership?
What are the most important leadership qualities? Can anyone learn how to become an effective leader and, if so, how are effective leaders born or made?

This book will dive into all these questions a lot more.

Let's begin by addressing this commonly asked question about whether it makes sense to invest one's time and energy in trying to become a more effective leader. Because if leaders are born with inherent qualities that can't be developed, why waste time in fighting a battle that's already been lost? Luckily, research demonstrates that leaders are "generally made." This intends that while there are parts of leadership that come more normally to certain individuals than to other people, a larger part of authority characteristics can be created. All in all, anybody can figure out how to be a successful leader. It requires responsibility and difficult work, yet it is conceivable. This is additionally uplifting news on the grounds that the most basic abilities for a leader have changed over the long haul.

Anyone can sit in a corner office and give out errands to be run, however there is something else to viable authority besides that. Successful leaders significantly affect the colleagues they make due, yet additionally their organization all in all. Representatives who work under incredible leaders will generally be more joyful, more useful and more associated with their association - and this has a gradually expanding influence that arrives at your business' primary concern.

> *"I think a great leader is one who makes those around them better,"* Dana Brownlee, founder of Professionalism Matters, told Business News Daily. *"There are many test for a great leader, but I really look to those around them: Are they growing? Becoming better leaders themselves? Motivated? And so on."*

If you look around and see that your team members have become disengaged or stagnant in their work, it may be time to revisit, recheck and reform your strategies.

A recent study by the Center for Creative Leadership showed that almost 38% to more than half of new leaders fail within their first 18 months. Leaders can avoid becoming part of this staggering statistic by incorporating good leadership strategies that motivate their team members to accomplish their goals. So let's go into YOU becoming a Great Leader

TABLE OF CONTENT.

- **INTRODUCTION**

- **CHAPTER ONE**
  WHO IS A LEADER.

- **CHAPTER TWO**
  LEADERS VS MANAGERS.

- **CHAPTER THREE**
  BECOMING A LEADER.

- **CHAPTER FOUR**
  LEADERS AND FOLLOWERS.

- **CHAPTER FIVE**
  AGE AND GENDER IN RELATION TO LEADERSHIP.

- **CONCLUSION**

CHAPTER ONE

WHO IS A LEADER?

We talk about leaders and leadership nearly every day in the business world and In all other areas of life, but have you ever tried to actually define leadership? It can be much harder than you may think, but taking the time to define leadership and what makes a leader is crucial to building a cohesive culture and developing future leaders. Many people struggled or had to pause to think because it's a word we use so frequently without really defining. We take the concept of leadership for granted and assume that we all know what leadership is and what a great leader looks like.

Who then is a Leader?
There have been countless people through history that led people but were inhumane and destructive. Does that still make them leaders? You can answer that. In my mind, a leader is someone who does more than just lead people. They have to be driven by the right motivation and make a positive impact on the people around them.

A leader is somebody who can perceive how things can be improved and who rallies individuals to push toward that better vision. Leaders pursue their vision and make it a reality while putting individuals first. A leader by its importance is one who goes first and shows others how its done, so others are persuaded to follow him. This is an essential prerequisite. To be a leader, an individual with high priority, has to establish himself and endeavor to accomplish his goals regardless of whether no one follows him! Just being able to motivate people isn't enough — leaders need to be empathetic and connect with people to be successful. Leaders don't have to come from the same background or follow the same path.

Future leaders will actually be more diverse, which brings a variety of perspectives. Of course, other people may not agree with my definition. The most important thing is that organizations are united internally with their definition of leadership.

What is Leadership?

Leadership involves knowledge, reliability, compassion, mental fortitude, and discipline.

- Leadership doesn't have anything to do with rank or one's situation in the progressive system of an organization.

Too many discussion about an organization's administration goes to the most senior leaders in the association. They are only that, Senior chiefs. Leadership doesn't naturally happen when you arrive at a specific compensation grade. Ideally you track down it there, however there are no assurances.

- Leadership has nothing to do with titles.

Similar to the point above, just because you have an high-level title, doesn't automatically make you a "leader." I'll always stress the fact that you don't need a title to lead. In fact, you can be a leader in your place of worship, your neighborhood, in your family, all without having a title.

According to U.S. academic environment "LEADERSHIP is a process of social influence in which a person can enlist the aid and support of others in the accomplishment of a common and ethical task". In my word I define Leadership as the potential to influence behaviour of others. It is also the capacity to influence a group towards the realization of a goal. Leaders are required to develop future visions, and to motivate the organizational members to want to achieve the visions.

So what then qualifies me to be a leader? This will be talk more on in coming chapters but let me talk on something we often attach to being a leader. It is called **AGE**.

I don't know if you've been assigned a task to do and then someone oppose that opinion due to the fact that you are not of an "old" age and you lose that opportunity to showcase your potential. It's painful right? Yeah, I can relate but wait does age makes one a good leader or at what age can one become a leader?

Let's talk about that in a short time. There has been a lot of talk on how age determines a lot of things In life even up to being a leader.

The short response is that age doesn't influence authority. Be that as it may, age assumes a part in administration viability, however not in the manner in which you could think. There are a few things that accompany age that can further develop your leadership abilities.

It is true that *"the older you get, the more life experience you gain,"* which is priceless for leadership. You learn what's important, how to handle conflict, how to prioritize, and more.

Asking whether age matters in administration are like asking as to whether height matters in sports. Surely a piece of your response relies upon the action and the position you take. Since the beginning of time, ladies and men of various ages have stood firm on administration situations. In any case, there are particular ages where certain individuals are preferable leaders over others on account of their experience and development. Here are some of the reasons why age matters:

- Age gives you point of view on things that occurred from quite a while ago. It's difficult to imagine others' perspective on the off chance that you've never been in theirs. Advanced age brings intelligence and information from disappointments.

- Age offers you the chance to fail a couple of times before you succeed, and that can give you significant knowledge into what works and what doesn't. This information will help you as a leader and assist with building trust with others since they see your devotion, responsibility, and versatility.

- Age assists individuals with taking analysis better. At the point when you're a more youthful individual, analysis can undoubtedly get under your skin or make you question yourself. Over the long haul, individuals foster a toughness since they gain from their missteps and sort out what they want. This makes it more straightforward for them to acknowledge useful analysis from others without being actually outraged or disturbed.

Now you have a clear understanding of how age affect leadership and this will be talk better on in coming chapters. Let me stop here and go into the next chapter.

CHAPTER TWO

LEADERS AND MANAGERS.

We've talked a bit about leaders in the first chapter. So we'll be talking more on managers and the difference between leaders and managers.

Managers assume a significant part in the general progress of an organization. They are liable for driving a group of representatives to meet objectives and accomplish execution measurements. If you have any desire to turn into a manager, it's useful to comprehend what the occupation resembles and a vocation you can take. In this chapter, we'll investigate the response to 'What/who is a manager?' How to become one and so on. Managers are often called different names such as directors, supervisor, Head of Team and so on.

Who is a Manager?

A manager is an expert who plays an influential role in an association and deals with a group of representatives. Frequently, managers are liable for dealing with a particular office in their organization. There are many kinds of managers, yet they as a rule have obligations like leading execution surveys and simply deciding. Managers are in many cases the line of correspondence between an organization's representatives and its significant level leaders.

A manager is also an expert in his or her field and serves as a support system for employees. Managers work within a business and work together as a team to achieve company goals. A manager is not a person who does a million things at once while employees take a back seat. It is vital for managers to give out tasks to employees and assist them if they need help.

Duties of a Manager.

As a manager you have to put on with many heats and be flexible. Imagine you are blindfolded and walking through a forest. Could you imagine how many times you would hit a tree or trip because you have no direction? You as a manager has to prevent your employees from such events. It is your job as a manager to help employees navigate. If they trip, it is the manager's job to help them stand up, re-strategise and motivate them to achieve their goals. A manager who watches his or her employee trip and fail without helping them is not the kind of manager you want to be.

A key responsibility of a manager is leading their team. They give direction to their employees and answer their questions. They also delegate tasks to specific employees and ensure that projects stay on track. Great managers commit to the role of being a fair leader to help increase their teams' productivity. Employees will feed off their manager's energy, and that positive energy will help create a successful work environment.

The role of a manager feels a great deal, the functions are many and varied, including:

1. Hiring and staffing.
2. Training new employees.
3. Coaching and developing existing employees.
4. Dealing with performance problems and terminations.
5. Supporting problem resolution and decision-making.
6. Conducting timely performance evaluations.
7. Translating corporate goals into functional and individual goals.
8. Monitoring performance and initiating action to strengthen results.
9. Monitoring and controlling expenses and budgets.
10. Tracking and reporting scorecard results to senior management.

LEADER vs MANAGER

Managers and Leaders have likenesses and contrasts. This should be visible through the jobs every individual plays in an association, business reconciliation, project arranging, human asset, and portion of obligations. In spite of recognizable similarities among the executives and authority. You should continuously keep in mind that very much likeness while looking at organization and the executives. After this, you will realize that any great manager can be a leader, yet not all leaders have the board abilities and qualities.

The key differences between a leader and Manager are as follow:

- A leader invents or innovates while a manager organizes

The leader of the team comes up with new innovations and tactics and kickstarts the organization's shift . A leader always has his or her eyes set on the great height, developing new techniques and strategies for the organization. A leader has immense knowledge of all the current trends, advancements, and skillsets—and has a clarity of purpose and vision. By contrast, a manager is someone who generally only maintains what is already established. A manager needs to watch the bottom line while supervising and overseeing employees and workflow in the organization and preventing any unfortunate events.

- A manager depends on control, though a leader moves trust:

A leader is an individual who pushes representatives to give their all and knows how to establish a suitable rhythm and beat until the end of the gathering. Managers, then again, are expected by their set of working responsibilities to lay out command over representatives, which, thus, assists them with fostering their resources for draw out their best. In this manner managers need to comprehend their subordinates wealthy their occupation successfully.

- A leader asks the questions "what" and "why", while a manager leans more towards the questions "how" and "when":

To be able to accomplish their role as a leader, some may question and challenge authority to modify or even change decisions that may not have the team's best interests in mind. Good leadership requires a great deal of good judgment, especially when it comes to the ability to stand up to superiors over a point of concern or if there is an aspect in need of improvement. If a company goes through a turbulent path, a leader will be the one who will stand up and ask the question: "What did we learn from this?" Managers, however, are not required to assess and analyze failures. Their job description stand more on asking the questions "how" and "when," which usually helps them make sure that plans are properly executed. They tend to accept the status quo exactly the way it is and do not attempt a change.

All this is just for you to know the difference between a Leader and a Manager so don't put it all together. Be A LEADER.

CHAPTER THREE

BECOMING A LEADER.

Everyone wants to be a leader but not everyone can pay the price. Some people are made leaders naturally while some have to groom their skills and deal with challenges and situations to get the peak of becoming a leader. Let me discuss little on whether Leaders are made or born. One of the most common questions when it comes to leadership is that are leaders born or made? Can leadership be developed or do leaders need to be genetically blessed with leadership traits? Eventually, the response is that both are correct: an individual can be brought into the world with normal leadership capacities, and somebody can figure out how to be a decent leader. Whether or not somebody is an "inborn leader," everybody has space to master new abilities and fill in administration capability.

    The capacity to prepare leaders is fantastic information for associations. You don't have to sit around idly for somebody with normal leadership abilities to show up — you can begin preparing incredible leaders today. Although some traits of great leaders may appear to be genetically passed, but leadership is a skill that can be learned. Even traits that are considered innate, such as creativity, can be groomed and enhanced. In some cases, many leaders do utilise natural, inherent traits. They may have developed key leadership traits due to the environments they were raised in, or may simply possess them naturally. For example, you might have come across leaders who are naturally influential. Without even trying or going extra miles, some leaders are able to inspire others, simply through their demeanour and presence.

But does that mean influencing is a native skill that leaders must be born with? No, it doesn't. Those who don't possess the skill have to obtain it in other ways, whether it be through training, mentorship or hands-on leadership experience. Now you know that you can learn to become a leader, you don't have to be born with the required skill. Even if you have the natural skill but don't utilise it, it's still a waste.

Traits of A Leader.

To have a broader picture of whether leaders are born or made, let's take a look at the top key traits of leaders.

Of course, this is only a brief list of top leadership traits that top key players possess. There are many more, but here we're focusing on what we believe are the most important leadership traits.

1. INFLUENCING

The best leaders are able to influence others. John C. Maxwell, a renowned leadership author and speaker, once states that *'leadership is influence'*. Some people may be able to influence others naturally, while others has to work on developing their influencing skills. Being a leader means you have followers and your followers are not just with you has moron but for a special purpose and the main reason while they are always with you is die to the influence you have in them. Let's take for example a football team, there are some players who perform excellently under a particular coach and when such coach leaves and another coach is brought in they find it hard under to adapt to that coach or his tactics and flop. Do we conclude that they are not talented or not good enough? No, the players are still the same but the influence of the past coach can't be easily rub off from them.

What are the ways of influencing people?

a) **Vision**

Why is vision important for leaders to influence people? Because it provides purpose. It shows teams where they're going and what they're investing their energy, time and substance in. When leaders provide an amazing vision, teams are inspired to work towards it. Vision can be learned and developed. Many leadership courses offer practical exercises to help leaders work on establishing vision and effectively conveying those visions to others
Top-tier leaders have a clear vision of their goals and where they want their company or project to go.

b) Confidence

To influence people and be a successful leader, confidence is a priority. Confident leaders believe in themselves and their visions, which encourages their followers to do the same, that is why those who are shy and easily frightened can't be leaders but congratulations, confidence is not something that all leaders are born with, it's a trait that is acquired and developed.

c) Communication

The majority of great leaders are also great communicators. This is mostly because good communication and interaction enables leaders to convey their visions, influence teams and gain trust. Although communication skills are often developed in the early years of our lives, the ability to communicate effectively is something that we can all develop over time. In fact, many leadership training offer courses that are specifically focused on communication. Improving your communication style can improve your ability to build relationships and influence others. Powerful leaders know when to talk and when to listen. They are effective communicators and are able to clearly explain to their employees everything from organizational goals to specific tasks. If people don't understand or aren't aware of your expectations, they will fall short, so the more specific you are, the more effective the work towards achieving the goals.

d) Producing great results under pressure

This is a massive trait that is expected of every Leaders to have. Learning to lead in a complex environment is a vital skill for any leader. Even before any definitive information is available, effective leaders must assess a situation's complexity and choose appropriate courses of action. A typical expertise of numerous incredible leaders is the capacity to keep calm and successfully lead when confronted with profoundly distressing, compressed circumstances. At the point when everyone around them lose confidence, the best leaders move forward and lead. This might appear as though an expertise that is natural, instead of learned. All things considered, how we answer complicated circumstances is frequently intuitive.
Notwithstanding, the abilities that leaders use to prevail under tension can be learned. For instance, leaders can foster their self-control by dealing with specific procedures. The capacity to prevail under tension can likewise be improved by acquiring active experience working in compressed circumstances.

e) Self-Management

If you can't manage yourself well It's going to be hard to manage others effectively. Self-managing means being able to make your goals the most important and being responsible for accomplishing those objectives. As an effective leader, it is expedient of you to utilize your time, attention and emotions, while remaining aware of your strengths, weaknesses and potential sources of bias. Exceptional leaders are adept at handling stress and balancing their private and professional lives. But you must also remember the importance of compassion and being cautious of how to respond to people and events in an appropriate way. Remember to maintain self-control and discipline in your actions, though you should avoid becoming overly reserved or inflexible.

Leaders exercise good self-control and regulation over their own behavior and are able to tolerate frustration and stress. Leaders are able to cope with changes in an environment without having an intense emotional reaction

f) Being Accountable And Responsible

Successful managers know how to use position and authority appropriately without overwhelming or overpowering employees. Effective leaders make themselves accountable and responsible for their own mistakes—and they expect others to be of the same attitude. They can work within established procedures, and be productive and efficient in their decisions. They appreciate the importance of support and encouragement give to individuals while also understanding organizational structures and the necessity to follow rules and policies. They are able to balance different perspectives while taking appropriate action. Leaders are ordinarily individuals situated around cooperative people. They're ready to encourage a group culture, include others in navigation, and show worry for each colleague. By being with arranged individuals, leaders can stimulate and persuade others. By causing every person to feel significant and indispensable to the group's prosperity, they secure the best endeavors from every individual from the group.

Roles of a Leader.

Leadership responsibilities are based on the type of business and industry the leader is associated with. All extraordinary leaders comprehend that their positions aren't straightforward. You don't start working, accomplish alot due to the work you did yesterday, and afterward shut it down for the day. The circumstances your association faces change consistently. This implies you really want to show the compelling authority abilities expected to handle significant issues.

Nonetheless, this isn't to imply that that there aren't normal obligations that all leaders should routinely embrace. They might be wide in definition, however these errands are fundamental assuming you are to lead really and make high-performing groups that come by results. There are several key duties of a good leader that span across all fields but the most essential and most important will be listed below:

- Keeping the vision alive.

You become a leader because you are the one who conceive the vision and bring it into reality. No one knows the vision better than you are so you are ressponsible for determining the goals that members will work toward.. When every other person give up on the vision, it is expedient of you to keep on moving to ensure the success of the vision. Leaders don't quit. You keep pushing on, you forget about the past achievement and focus on the future ahead of you. When all odds are against you, you brace up yourself to challenge and overcome them. Remember that "once your vision dies, you also die." Bringing visions into reality isn't a days job, it is like planting a seed into a tree. It requires a lot of energy, consistency, commitment, time, money and whatever you might think of and if care is not taken you might easily give up. But learn this "before a tree is seen, the seed has to die." This is not a naturally death but during the death, it spring forth into a new life, so when it seems like the vision is not becoming what you want it to be, keep weeding and watering.

- Be a role model.

Leaders lead by example. What you express and display is what your subordinates will do. The environment you create for your followers is what will motivate them to work and believe in you. The energy you give out is the energy your people will receive. A leader should be a mentor that provides the mentee with the foundation to be successful. This type of leader is the perfect asset to have when reaching new heights in any area of life. Team members often follow the work ethic of the team leader. Some team members will need more help than others, but it's important that you show you have that level of interest in everyone around you to keep morale and interest high. Displaying confidence in your vision and the team itself can help to instill confidence in your followers. A leader who has integrity is not only more likely to be trusted by their team members but also will often be respected and appreciated by the team.

- Supervision of Daily Activities

A key responsibility of a leader in a business, industry or in any field is overseeing the daily activities of his staffs or followers. This typically includes scheduling, assigning tasks, developing work flow charts and project plans. It may also involve setting goals with individual employees and helping them secure the tools and resources necessary to perform their jobs to the best of their abilities. A decent leader will help other people foster their expert abilities and skills. This incorporates tutoring, position shadowing and appointing properly expanding levels of liability to qualified representatives. It is also expected of leaders to act as a sounding board for workers, sharing information with guidance and supporting proceeding with schooling and expert turn of events. Furthermore, compelling leaders will help representatives in investigating work issues, dealing with risky clients and assisting them with zeroing in on the positive parts of their presentation.

- Conflict Management

Many leaders are tasked with investigating and judging interoffice disputes between colleagues. This can involve the responsibilities of listening to employee concerns, putting into note problematic areas and helping staffers resolve workplace issues. Besides, the responsibility of a leader is to act as the first line of defence between employees and customers when problems arise, helping to mitigate damage and smooth over customer service issues. Leaders are assigned to reprove and train workers when essential. The interaction commonly incorporates liabilities like advising, laying out progress objectives and circling back to trouble spots. In the occasion a representative showcases persistent degrees of amateurish way of behaving or horrible showing, a leader is likewise confronted with the choice to end a laborer contract when essential. In becoming a leader, always act with integrity. Establish a business code of conduct for your subordinates and lead by example. Effective leaders establish an atmosphere of trust and fairness. Developing expertise in this core competency prepares a leader to promote and value diversity, adhere to local, state and federal regulations and ensure workers safety.

DO'S AND DON'T OF A LEADER

As it is expected of everyone to live by rules and principles, it also how's the same to a leader even not more important. A leader is always at the does front to his/her followers and that ultimately put him as the mirror of the vision, organization or industry in which whosoever is behind him/her looks up to. The following are the key principles essential for a great leader to adhere to.

1) Lead by example.

You'll request that your group keep an exclusive requirement, so put forth certain that you're giving similar attempt as they are. Ensure you're in on time, do your fair share, and do your portion of the work. It's a lot simpler to regard somebody who will joyfully contribute all to the others. You'll likewise have a superior thought of what it resembles to deal with a task, so you'll be more sensible in your requests. Your mentality will come off in your group. Okay, imagine it, who will help you have an improved outlook on coming to work: somebody who's downbeat and skeptical, or somebody who's cheery and amped up for the current task? You know the answer already. *"A decent leader realizes that they set the vibe for work,"* says expert Benjamin Davids at Academized, *"The more you work to raise their group's spirits, the better that group will do."*

2) Don't isolate yourself.

Always remember that you are at the front and others are behind, you may see ahead clearly but there are others who can see what's going on behind you clearly than you do. Some leaders try and keep themselves from the rest of the organization, as they feel they can do it all. They may also isolate themselves from their own team, out of a sense of self-importance. Doing this means that they're missing out on help and key information from other workers, and actually weakening their own team.

There's a demeanor in certain organizations that feelings

ought to be kept out of the working environment. To a degree, this is valid, yet everybody has sentiments about each part of their work. It's an ill-conceived notion to excuse any of your group's sentiments impromptu. Make time to pay attention to them, and follow up on them if fundamental. Keep in mind, your colleagues are not robots. You and your employees should have mutual respect for each other. Many leaders get carried away in being "the big boss" and forget that their employees are just as important to the ultimate goal(s) as they are. Remember, the gift of men is extremely important to any leader's success.

3) Communicate easily with your followers.

    Just like in a relationship, communication is essential. As long as you are a leader, you are already in a relationship with everyone supporting your vision or whatsoever you're working on. Most of the communication that happens in the workplace is now through the written word i.e emails and memos. After all, how many more emails do you get now compared to phone calls? Therefore, your writing skills are very important. You've got to be clear in all the communications that you make. Your team should be able to read an email and know exactly what you need from them. This means that whatever you're sending, you need to go through it over and over again so has to prevent the misinterpretations of words. To be a good leader, you should make time to proofread these communications. If time is too tight to do this, you can enlist the help of professionals. But it should be necessary done by you you because no one knows it better that you.

4) Don't play the blame game.

Be ready to face the consequences. Whatever you do, don't blame your mistakes on your employees. While you should be holding them accountable for their mistakes, it's just as important to hold yourself accountable for yours. In the event that things turn out badly, awful leaders pin the issue in their group without checking the master plan out. This causes hatred, and things can rapidly go bad. All things considered, take a check at what everyone might have improved, including yourself. Request criticism from your group and utilize the examples figured out how to work on from here on out.

When there's an error, don't just vent your anger on anyone you see or pour out your frustrations on your followers instead take the time to sit down with them and find out what it is they don't understand or where you all get it wrong. From there, teach them how to fix it and also learn how you can avoid such mistakes again.

5) Be positive and optimistic.

A leader has the greatest faith and believe In whatsoever he/she plans and set out. Great Leaders are continuously contemplating the future, and searching for choices that might open up to them. Assuming that you're keeping one foot from here on out, you can make the most of chances as they emerge, and be ready for any issues that come your direction. They likewise take guidance from others, including their group, about how they think ought to be arranged ahead of time. On the off chance that you're reluctant to commit errors, your group will be as well. This implies that they'll face less challenges, finish less, and offer short of what they would have in any case. It's greatly improved to work as well as could be expected, and when the mix-ups occur, gain from them and continue on.

A leader with an heightened belief system will only want to take risk because he believes 100% In it. Yes, every good leader takes calculated risks. Whether it's trusting an employee with a project out of their comfort zone or taking a mental health day, trusting your gut and taking risks is important. Your role is to support and lead your team in a way that produces results. It is not unusual to be fearful during this transition. But if you allow that fear to run the show you'll start behaving in ways that limit team and individual performances. Anxiety doesn't focus on our ability to try and overcome challenges, instead, it focuses on limiting beliefs and staying safe. This is the self-protective side of fear which is great if you're hiding in a cave from a wild animal, but not so helpful in a corporate environment! Fear usually minimises opportunity and options to create less risk. Leadership is risky, so acknowledge your fear but don't let it control your behaviour.

6) Don't do it all.

A tree doesn't make a forest, it only start it. Yes you are the leader, boss and you know the vision with the right strategies to make it work out but sometimes you have to take the pedal away from your foot and give others to lead the line. Delegate tasks to your group, make them feel among and not inferior. Let them know you appreciate and acknowledge them, give them a chance to lead and access their strength and weakness. A few leaders are sure, possibly by mistake, that the very thing that they need to say is a higher priority than whatever else. The inverse is valid, truth be told. A decent leader is all the more a facilitator, uniting every other person's thoughts and making them work as one. Expect to listen more than you talk. I urge you to zero in on how you enhance your administrative role. This will mean various things at various timea because some of the time your job will be to help others to succeed, and at different times it implies introducing your thoughts, getting others ready and making change.

In the last part of this chapter we'll be talking about the various type of leaders/leadership hat exist and you can pick the one that best fit you so follow till the end.

VARIETIES OF LEADERSHIP.

Different working environments demand different styles of leadership, and great leaders typically combine characteristics of many different leadership types to manage effectively. With regards to what's happening in the association, leaders are either getting it going (positive or negative), permitting it to work out (fortunate or unfortunate), or keeping it from working out (positive or negative). Eventually, the top chief is dependable, regardless of whether they acknowledge liability.

High-influence, groundbreaking leaders know this and get a sense of ownership with all that is going on. In the interim, low-influence leaders abstain from getting a sense of ownership with what's going on as they look for others to fault. They make a huge measure of doubt all through the association as they attempt to keep up with power and control. It takes an extremely serious level of character to make the progress to turn into a high-influence leader, since you should move past just tolerating liability regarding developing yourself. At the point when you genuinely — and truly — decide to start to develop and foster others, you should become dependable to other people. Low-influence leaders are reluctant to do this and change their sort of administration style. They have the capacity, yet they don't have the longing. The following are the varieties of leadership you can style with or choose to be.

1) **Transactional Leadership.**

Transactional Leadership originates from the thought that work and explicit ventures are an exchange: When a representative acknowledges a task, he/she consents to "comply" to the leader and complete the undertakings and obligations as doled out, and will be remunerated in return for her endeavors. Laborers might be compensated or rebuffed in light of their presentation.

Jobs are distinct, and individuals who are aggressive and answer rewards are probably going to do well under this sort of administration. Moreover, this initiative style lays out an obviously characterized structure that empowers the association to meet transient objectives. In any case, value-based authority doesn't consider a lot of development or imagination in representatives. It likewise lays out an unbending design that may not answer well to change. The best way to understand transactional leadership is to view a typical transaction of trade by barter or give and take. That is really the basis of this leadership style. Transactional leaders dish out instructions to their team members and then use different rewards and penalties to either recognize or punish what they do in response.

You Might Be a Transactional Leader If...

- You regularly utilize the danger of remaining late when you really want to propel your group.

- You're continually conceptualizing eyes catching ways of perceiving strong work — your group are anxiously waiting to see what you think of after last month's taco party.

2) **Autocratic Leadership.**

Autocratic leaders, otherwise called dictator leaders, by and large have all the power, authority, and obligation in an association. This style of leadership is the opposite side of democratic leadership. There is seldom information or dynamic in the piece of group or gathering individuals; all things considered, colleagues are entrusted with executing the leader's choices and decisions. You can think of this as a "my way or the highway" approach. This kind of authority is extremely unbending, however in circumstances that request structure, fast navigation, and close oversight, it very well may be helpful to the association. There are likewise numerous traps: the association can't work without the leader, communication might be defective or lacking, and members might feel unsettled.

You Might Be an Autocratic Leader If...

- You think group conversations and conceptualizing just slow things down, and it's better in the event that you go with significant choices alone.

- You disdain it when representatives question your choices — when you've said something, that is conclusive.

3) **Transformational Leadership.**

This leadership style says it all in the name. Transformational leaders seek to change (I mean, transform) the businesses or groups in which they lead by inspiring their employees to innovate. People under this style of leadership have tons of autonomy, plenty of breathing room to innovate and think outside the box. This style doesn't need the leader to be available to impact change, on the grounds that the leader starts change through the association and persuades workers to perform. They are the most influential of the types of leaders and are highly respected. Their reputation precedes them. They are well known for developing leaders. They have influenced many leaders for many years. Their influence is continuously being transferred through many other leaders at many different times in multiple locations.

Transformational Leadership requests an elevated degree of efficiency and contribution from representatives. While this style can go quite far in affecting genuine change, it might abuse a few representatives to the hindrance of others. Transformation leaders additionally risk setting too-high assumptions for colleagues.

You Might Be a Transformational Leader If...

- You take a look at each and every current cycle with an insightful eye and a solid sense that it very well may be better.

- You're continuously reassuring others to get outside their usual ranges of familiarity and stretch their own boundaries.

- You could overflow with satisfaction at whatever point you see a colleague accomplish something recently remembered to be unimaginable.

4) **Democratic Leadership.**

This is also know as Participative Leadership, all or most group individuals can partake in dynamic cycles. Democratic leaders stress uniformity and empower conversation and a progression of thoughts.

This style of leadership generally can be a viable administration style and has various advantages — it empowers imagination, underlines reasonableness, and values knowledge and trustworthiness — there are a few likely downsides. Jobs might be less distinct, which could bring about correspondence issues and disappointments. Some group individuals, normally those with less experience, might be less willing or ready to contribute, or feel that their commitments are not however esteemed as others may be.

You Might Be a Democratic Leader If...

- You think the best gatherings are the ones where everybody has an equivalent opportunity to make an appearance.

- You can't recollect the last time you settled on a significant choice without getting input from undoubtedly another individual.

5) **Laissez-faire Leadership**

Representatives of Laissez-faire leaders have a serious level of independence. In this Leadership style, leaders keep a hands-off way to deal with overseeing laborers, furnishing them with the devices they need to take care of their business without being straightforwardly associated with dynamic cycles and day to day undertakings with obligations. As it may, these leaders actually get a sense of ownership with the organization's choices, despite the fact that the ability to settle on these choices rests in the possession of the representatives. The laissez-faire leadership style can be successful when employees are skilled in the nature of the work and motivated to succeed. Workers enjoy independence, which may be appealing to many employees. This type of leadership can have consequences when the leader is uninvolved or takes a passive approach to working with employees who need more guidance. It can also lead to a lack of unity and cohesion in a group or team, and projects may fall off track without strong oversight.

You Might Be a Laissez-Faire Leader If...

- You scarcely do any of the talking in project group gatherings. All things considered, your colleagues are the ones updating you on where things are.

- You're truly just associated with most assignments and ventures at two central issues: the start and the end.

I know by now you know the type of leader you are and you might be asking yourself, how can I change from one style of leadership to another and if it is possible? Perhaps you're a transactional leader and want to be more transformational, or you think you could incorporate more Autocratic leadership into your existing style.

The good news is You absolutely can change your personal leadership style. *"Your leadership style isn't a paid annual membership,"* says Crawford. Changing your leadership style is actually fairly straightforward in concept (although it might be difficult in practice), and you can do it at any time. The key is to cautiously check out your ineffective habits for new ones that are more in line with the style you want to inculcate, and *"stay committed to practicing your new leadership style and technique."*

In the event that you're battling to try and sort out how you can be more successful or what the best administration style for you is in any case, Padua suggests that you start by contemplating a leader or mentor you respected. *"What were their characteristics?" "How did they respond? What did they say? How could it affect you?"* That exercise can assist you with distinguishing a characteristics that you might want to carry out in your own style

However, there's no such thing as a "perfect" leadership style, leadership isn't one size fits all. All of these varieties come with their benefits and disadvantages, and some of them will be more effective in certain scenarios. Notwithstanding where you think your own ongoing style fits in, there are possibilities a couple of changes you can make to be much more compelling. Like anything, leadership is a growing experience, and it takes a tad of experimentation to hit the nail on the head.

"Don't hesitate for even a moment to commit errors," says Crawford. *"That is the manner by which we learn. Once in a while you might need to take a couple of attempts at various styles to make things work. Be kind with yourself."*

CHAPTER FOUR

LEADERS AND FOLLOWERS

Leaders matter incredibly. In any case, in looking so passionately for better leaders we generally neglect to focus on individuals these leaders lead. In the event that you have not heard the expression "followership" before, or not brood over it, you are in good company. It generally shows up as a "non-word" when reports are spell-kept an eye on the PC. It's anything but another idea — only one that is frequently ignored or neglected.

Why followership is ignored is a fascinating idea. Without supporters, could there be leaders? Who might they lead? Who might turn into the leaders on the off chance that they were not first the devotees? Leadership and followership is a steady bond: Leaders rely upon devotees as well as the other way around. Consider it: Without his armed forces, all things considered, Napoleon was only a man with intense desires. Associations and ventures succeed or flop mostly based on how well their leaders lead, yet somewhat additionally on how well their supoorters follow. In the expressions of one famous undertaking leader: *"Task supervisors are not great leaders; colleagues are not really compelling supporters. Many managers couldn't lead a pony to water. Many subordinates couldn't follow a motorcade. Certain individuals stay away from one or the other job. Others acknowledge the job push onto them and perform it ineffectively."* Leadership and followership are closely related. Effective followers can sharpen productive leadership behavior just as effective leaders develop employees into good followers. In this book, we examine the important role of effective followership, including the nature of the followers' role, different styles of followership that individuals express, and how effective followers behave. We also explore how followers develop personal potential to be more effective. We also look at what followers want from leaders and examine the leader's role in developing effective followers through feedback and coaching.

Associations train individuals in administration as well as followership jobs. Organizations are empowering leaders to be more certifiable and credible. We should not fail to remember there is a leader, a follower, and a third component — the relationship. Leading in the new frontier will expect people to concentrate on the unique job of the study of the connection between the leader and supporter. Followership is significant in the conversation of leadership in light of multiple factors. Without supporters there are no leaders. For any venture or association to succeed, there should be individuals who enthusiastically and actually follow, similarly as there should be the people who energetically and successfully lead. Leadership and followership are central jobs that people shift into and out of under different circumstances. Everybody — leaders included — is a follower at some time. For sure, most people, even those in, influential places, have a boss of some sort or another. People are more frequently supporters than leaders. Large numbers of the necessary skills in leaders are similar characteristics required in compelling supporters. As well as having drive, freedom, obligation to shared objectives, and fortitude, a supporter can offer excited help of a leader, yet not to the degree that a supporter neglects to challenge a leader who is dishonest or undermines the qualities or targets of the association. We accept that inadequate followers are as a lot to fault for lackluster showing, moral and legitimate slips inside associations so also are poor and unscrupulous leaders. Supporters have an obligation to make some noise when leaders do things wrong.

Everyone wants to be a leader. You get to make the key decisions, get the most credit when things go well, get the blame when things go wrong. Yet few people understand that to be a good leader, you first need to be a great follower. As Aristotle said, *"He who cannot be a good follower, cannot be a good leader."*

Who is a follower?

This is a conspicuous inquiry in conversations about execution in the labor force, on the grounds that the view held when the term fellower is utilized is that supporters are compliant and assume a subordinate part. They are individuals who are some way or another seen as shoddy. From youth, our emphasis has been on being a leader and has coordinated consideration away from the significance of following. However no task or coordinated exertion can succeed or be supported without followers. Consider a tactical situation. Without great subordinates, the military couldn't achieve their essential military objectives. Neither might a games at some point group dominate matches in the event that everybody chose to be the leader. Every individual assumes an indispensable part. The commitment, everything being equal, who might have different ranges of abilities, to high-performing sports, military or undertaking groups is undeniable. Excellent work can't finish without great supporters.

Things to know as an Follower:

I define followership as the willingness to cooperate in working toward the accomplishment of the mission, to demonstrate a high degree of teamwork and to build cohesion among the organization members. There are few talks on guiding one to be an effective follower, though there are some. Let's get to them.

1) You are a Leader-in-Training

The best supporters don't consider themselves to be one more pinion in the corporate hardware. They understand what they're doing. They understand what their companions are doing. They even understand what their leaders are doing. They know since they need to be aware. They need to know since leaders should know more than every other person.

Believe it or not, leaders. Not followers. The best followers aren't actually followers. They see themselves as future leaders. And they have already started their own personal leadership journey. They happen to be self-leaders who follow. Once you see yourself like this, you don't see yourself as someone of a low status but one becoming a great person in time to come.

2) Put your team first.

The best supporters are likewise the best cooperative individuals. They know one truth: they are just as good as their group. Furthermore, prepare to have your mind blown. Their leaders know that about them and feel extremely grateful for them. At the point when you make individual penances to ultimately benefit the group, you're communicating the message, *"I care about 'us' more than 'me'."* That kind of benevolence barely at any point slips by everyone's notice and undervalued. Cooperative followers are the "glue" that holds the group together. Their leaders count on them. Their peers confide in them. Everyone else likes them. How does this helps you as a future leader? Guess who else puts the team first? That's right, a good leader.

3) Believe in yourself and your leader.

The best followers really trust their capacities and the capacities of their leadees. They needn't bother to be determined what to do, how to make it happen, and when to do it. They simply finish things. They likewise know, and expect, that their leaders will finish things as well. A common trust keeps the work motor murmuring along pleasantly. As a decent follower, you have the boldness and certainty to deferentially examine with your leader in the event that you accept you're not heading down the correct path. You believe that your leader would see the value in the soul of your feedback and commitment. To be a successful leader in the future, you will need competent and confident followers. Legendary adman David Ogilvy once said, *"If each of us hires people who are bigger than we are, we shall become a company of giants."*

4) Follow what you belief, not who.

Don't be shock. The best followers don't simply follow a leader; they follow the leader's main goal or vision. The leader is nevertheless an encapsulation of that reason. Mac's workers might have adored the notable Steve Jobs, yet it's his vision and Apple's central goal in light of development and plan that makes them genuine supoorters and followers. Supporters become die-hard promoters when their own energy and object are lined up with those of their leaders. As a leader, you will actually want to see yourself as something more to a supporter and promoter of a mission, one that is a lot greater than you. Such a perspective will allow you the humility to see past yourself and focus on your vision and execution.

There's nothing wrong with being a great follower. Especially when you're following with leadership intent. What you learn as a follower can prepare you to be a greater leader than you could ever have imagined.

QUALITIES OF A GOOD FOLLOWER

Just like there are characters that define a good leader so also are qualities that define a good follower. Just so you know, followers are the bedrock for the success of any vision, organization or industry. A leader can't do it all so there comes the importance of a good follower, therefore there are qualities that define a good follower.

1) Self Management.

   The way to being a powerful follower is the capacity to have an independent perspective — to practice control and autonomy and to work without close management. Great followers are individuals to whom a leader can securely designate liability, individuals who expect needs at their own degree of skill and authority.
One more part of this oddity is that compelling followers see themselves — besides with regards to line liability — as the equivalents of the leaders they follow. They are more apt to openly disagree with leadership and less likely to be intimidated by hierarchy and organizational structure. At the same time, they can see that the people they follow are, in turn, following the lead of others, and they try to appreciate

the goals and needs of the team and the organization. Ineffective followers, on the other hand, succumb into the hierarchy and, seeing themselves as pawn, vacillate between despair over their seeming powerlessness and attempts to manipulate leaders for their own purposes.

Of course not all leaders like having self-managing followers. Some would rather have "sheep" or yes people. The best that good followers can do in this situation is to protect themselves and to stay attractive in the marketplace. The qualities that make a good follower are too much in demand to go begging for long.

2) Commitment.

Effective followers are committed to commodity — a cause, a product, an association, an idea — in addition to the care of their own lives and careers. Some leaders misinterpret this commitment. Seeing their authority conceded, they mistake fidelity to a thing for infidelity to themselves. But the fact is that numerous effective followers see leaders simply as coadventurers on a good campaign, and if they suspect their leader of flagging commitment or clashing motives they may just withdraw their support, either by changing jobs or by contriving to change leaders. The opportunities and the dangers posed by this kind of commitment are visible.

On the one hand, commitment is contagious. Most people like working with colleagues whose hearts are in their work.

Thier morale stays high, workers who begin to wander from their purpose are jostled back into line, projects stay on track and on time. In addition, an appreciation of commitment and the way it works can give leaders an extra tool with which to understand and channel the energies and loyalties of their subordinates.

Effective followers always give their beat and their loyalties to satisfy organizational needs. Effective leaders know how to channel the energies of strong commitment in ways that will satisfy corporate goals as well as a follower's personal needs.

3) Competence and Focus.

Because committed inadequacy is still ineptitude, powerful followers ace abilities that will be helpful to their associations. They hold better execution principles than the workplace requires, and proceeding with learning is natural to them, a staple in their expert turn of events. Less compelling followers anticipate that preparation and improvement should come to them. The main instruction they procure is always given. Their ability weakens except if some leader offers them parental consideration and consideration.

Great followers take on additional work readily, however first they make a heavenly showing off on their center liabilities. They are great judges of their own assets and shortcomings, and they contribute well to groups. Requested to act in regions where they are ineffectively qualified, they make some noise. Like competitors extending their abilities, they wouldn't fret risking disappointment assuming they realize they can succeed, however they are mindful so as to save the organization squandered energy, lost time, and lackluster showing by acknowledging demands that colleagues are more ready to meet. Great followers see colleagues as partners as opposed to contenders.

At the same time, effective followers often search for overlooked problems. For example, a woman on a new product development team discovered that no one was responsible for coordinating engineering, marketing, and manufacturing. She worked out an interdepartmental review schedule that identified the people who should be involved at each stage of development. Instead of burdening her boss with yet another problem, this woman took the initiative to present the issue along with a solution.

4) Courage.

Powerful followers are valid, fair, and bold. They set up a good foundation for themselves as free, basic scholars whose information and judgment can be relied upon. They pay some respect, conceding errors and sharing victories. They structure their own perspectives and moral norms and go to bat for what they trust in. Quick, real, and courageous, they can keep leaders and associates alert and aware and informed. The opposite side of the coin obviously is that they can likewise bring incredible hardship for a leader with problematic morals. Followers must be courageous enough to confront and challenge the leaders especially when the leader is derailing from the core values and vision.

THE LEADER-FOLLOWER RELATIONSHIP

The great philosopher Aristotle once said, *"He who cannot be a good follower, cannot be a good leader."* Would there be leaders without followers, and would these leaders be "leaders" if they had not initially been followers? Both positions are equally important, require responsibility, and interact with each other: the leader must help his followers grow, whereas the followers must contribute to the success of their leader. A leader impacts his group, similarly as a group makes effect on a leader. This joint effort can be both positive and negative, impacted by the capacity of the two players to trust, tune in, help, tackle issues and track down new arrangements. Both effectively executing and effectively making due, managing, and animating these positions guarantees viable joint effort among followers and leaders. Achieving organization objectives advances collaboration of followers and leaders in directing their group toward the organization objectives. Each organization has huge personalities who are prepared to not just oversee and screen the cycles inside the organization yet additionally to really execute and carry out them. Likewise, people who are talented in giving powerful division of work to each colleague are expected to convey the result as effective as could be expected and in accordance with every individual's abilities and capacities.

Every leader was once a follower. Each leader has been

essential for a group of followers who has demonstrated his capacity and power to achieve explicit errands through his commitment and energy. In any case, that doesn't imply that they are fit for driving all work processes. So everybody in the organization has their own singular methodology for doing various positions and tackling issues, and that implies that anybody can turn into an innovator in a specific undertaking for however long they are willing and prepared to assume responsibility.

Leaders and followers are impacted by one another.
    Leaders impact their followers through the organization's requirements, while followers impact leaders with their mentality and activities - it can have both positive and adverse consequences. This common impact of the two sides is a bringing together component that can work on the presentation and efficiency of both the leader and the colleagues. Every employee of the company is essential to ensure full functionality, regardless of its position. Both leaders and followers are a united team that interacts with each other, proving the need for their mutual collaboration to perform their jobs effectively. In a general sense, a decent Leader - Follower Relationship (LFR) is about trust, receptiveness and regard. It goes a lot farther than just causing no damage or harm to individuals inside their work space. A decent LFR is one that addresses genuine coordinated effort between the accomplices in and considers both the worth given and the worth acquired by both.

A tree doesn't make a forest, just like a leader can't achieve it all. You might think your vision is a personal one and wouldn't want to include people, how true it is can also be disastrous because every personal vision will one day turn to a corporate vision to be able to achieve its global aims and objectives. Start acknowledging your followers, don't ridicule them, they are instrumental to your success and to the accomplishment of your vision.

- **START BUILDING YOUR LEADER-FOLLOWERS RELATIONSHIP.**

CHAPTER FIVE

AGE AND GENDER IN RELATION TO LEADERSHIP.

Just like described in the first chapter about the connection of age with Leadership, this chapter will give a broad knowledge about the connection of age, gender and leadership.

Age and Leadership.

With regards to administration, age doesn't make any difference - competency does. History is full with instances of leaders who have succeeded and fizzled at each age. The intangibles of energy, character, responsibility, wisdom, and ability are of boundlessly more noteworthy significance than somebody's date of birth. I couldn't care less about your generational class, however I in all actuality do think often about your capacity to contribute. In most countries around the world, the population is rapidly aging. The result of this is that older adults will likely occupy more positions of power and leadership in our societies than ever before. Further, cultural differences might shape how these transitions unfold around the globe. Psychological research has put it that older leaders have some distinctive qualities compared to younger leaders, in review to this a field study was conducted to examine this issue and it was revealed that more older leaders had the option to create prevalent objective execution (i.e., number of deals) among their subordinates contrasted with more youthful pioneers. The analysis hypothesized that one justification for this impact might be that in some exhibition based settings, for example, deals and contracts, more leaders advanced in age can display prevalent execution for their subordinates, which, thus, supports their efficiency. In 2008, a researcher named Kennedy continue the research and found that age moderated the relationship between transformational leadership(comprised of charisma, inspirational motivation, intellectual stimulation) and the group performance with the end goal that transformational Leadership is bound to emphatically affect group performance when the leader is more older than the colleagues. These discoveries recommend a relationship among age and leadership, with more older leaders taken as a wellspring of motivation by their groups.

However, research has also shown that there may be important drawbacks to having older individuals leading team members who are significantly younger than them. For example, age difference may lead to low job satisfaction via poor communication channels between older leaders and younger followers, as well as high role-ambiguity coming from contrast in how older and younger individuals view the nature of work and their responsibilities. Moreover, greater age difference between a senior mentor and a young follower is related to decreased agreement in their views of the partnership, likely due to meaningful differences in desires and goals from the mentorship aspect. In spite of the fact that age distinctions among leaders and their supporters truly do without a doubt deliver some regular rubbing toward the start of the relationship, this strain is decreased over the long run, and frequently killed as people come to be aware and figure out each other in additional significant ways, rather than making decisions in view of shallow qualities like age.

Also, research has shown that age differences among leaders and their followers shouldn't be guaranteed to create pressure, but instead this relationship is many times subject to extra factors, for example, how more youthful followers view older people all the more for the most part.

DOES AGE AFFECT LEADERSHIP?

We continually develop personally thus does our leadership abilities. Leadership capacities find opportunity to create. When a worker gives indications of potential to be a leader, mentors need to step in and begin directing them into a viable leader. Leadership knows no age, race, or orientation. Administration capacities just sparkle whenever offered the right chance. Circumstances can once in a while introduce brilliantly and with the right undertaking and at these minutes individuals can show their natural capacities to lead,

Ideally it shouldn't. Senior or more established leaders bank on demonstrated methodologies and activity plans while more youthful, more junior leaders face challenges with fresher plans achieved by considering new ideas. Despite age, administration capacities ought not be decided by age. The old leaders need to figure out how to adjust quicker, welcome change, and pay attention to the market patterns. While the you doing leaders should think about the senior leaders' perspectives and ideas since they have been in the business sufficiently long to settle on choices as a matter of fact.

However, let's consider how age affect leadership.

- Being experienced and old enough has its upsides and downsides in being a leader and particularly in the leadership capacities and characteristics that one has. Be that as it may, we should take a look at the upsides and downsides of having old people as leaders.

THE UPSIDES:

Intelligence - As a seasoned leader, you have the insight to make great, sound, and firm choices. You know the market/industry well indeed and can foresee the result of specific choices because of this experience.

Firm - A senior leader doesn't turn out to be effectively influenced with patterns and unforeseen changes on the lookout. A developed leader banks on demonstrated and compelling measures in handling or running the organization.

Steadfastness - Staying with the organization for quite a long time and climbing from the positions shows reliability. Makes a decent good example for the more youthful age, the more youthful heads of the organization.

DOWNSIDES:

Resistant to change - Old leaders in organizations are the most challenging to persuade that change is essential. They immovably trust that " if it isn't broken, for what reason should you fix it?" It requires investment for them to acknowledge the chance of changing conventions and strategies.

Challenged in adjusting - Once the requirement for change is acknowledged, there can trouble in adjust to it. There is an expressing "difficulty to impart new habits when old ones are so deeply ingrained." In the business world, it isn't showing the senior leaders how to change but how to go about it in tolerating each part of the change that is occurring.

Trouble in giving up - Senior leaders stay ready for quite a while just on the grounds that they feel great in the job and are not ready to continue on toward another really difficult job. They likewise could find it hard to pass the obligation of the job to a more youthful leader expecting that a more younder leader might not have the experience to 'handle the intensity'.

- Exactly the same thing in being a youthful leader. As a youthful leader, your choices and activities are dependably on the radar of the seniors in the organization. There is a consistent requirement for a young leader to promote as well as upgrade their leadership abilities for them to get their situation in the organization. More youthful leaders are intense and bold and more often than not they shock the organization, the board, the labor force since they either meet and surpass assumptions or they fizzle. Be that as it may, more often than not, different areas of the organization anticipate that more young leaders should fall flat. Let's talk about the advantages and disadvantages of having a young leader.

ADVANTAGES:

New Ideas - A youthful leader in many cases has creative thoughts. This is on the grounds that they are so used to considering new ideas. Not simply agreeing to what is compelling and what is working. These youthful leaders show that they move and think quick by assessing cycles and methodology consistently.

Always current - More youthful leaders can be more mindful of the most recent patterns and what is hot. They discuss patterns, talk about potential responses, concoct groundbreaking thoughts and activity plans. They are so enthusiastic and confident that they frequently feel a sense of urgency to think of projects and assessments to source out data that might develop the organization which is so essential for an organization's prosperity.

Competitive - Young leaders are known to be serious which drives them to succeed while high rank leadwrs can become careless in their job.

DISADVANTAGES:

Excessively serious - On occasion, more youthful leaders are excessively competitive and can underestimate representative experience and unwaveringness, maybe failing to remember that experienced leaders have had long periods of contest and are where they are as a result of their wise expertise, capacities and abilities.

Excessively aggressive - Youth gives trust, that is the thing they say. Nonetheless, when the more youthful leaders hurry into choices and arranging, this may on occasion be excessively hazardous or excessively exorbitant for the organization

Validity - A youthful leader's capacity and validity would continuously be addressed, and ventures might be more challenging to get endorsed. This can make a youthful leader, more aggressive, to convince upper administration to face challenges. They have something to demonstrate while additional developed supervisors have had direct insight to base their judgment and choices from.

I hope you can answer the question yourself now when ask the question if age matters in being leader. Now let's talk about Gender and Leadership.

GENDER AND LEADERSHIP.

The subject of leadership has been tended to and applied for centuries. However, it is just beyond 80 years that leadership has been a subject of serious conversation. It is essential to comprehend factors applicable to successful leadership. Orientation is one such factor that should be analyzed with respect to enhancing administration viability. The subject of orientation and authority merits serious and smart thought and conversation in light of expert, political, social, and individual real factors of the twenty-first 100 years. Women and men have been, are, and ought to be leaders. Orientation should be considered to decide how every leader can arrive at greatest potential and adequacy.

Men and women will generally settle on the overall significance of the top level of leadership characteristics. In spite of the fact that ladies put to some degree more significance on knowledge and genuineness than men. Bigger orientation holes arise on a portion of the other, and less significant qualities. Ladies are substantially more possible than men to say that being caring is significant in a leader in relation to 66% of ladies and 47% of men. Ladies likewise put a higher worth on development than men do. Some 61% of ladies believe this characteristic to be significant in being a leader, contrasted to 51% of men. The public sees little differentiation among men and women on few of these Leadership qualities. Vast larger parts say that with regards to knowledge and advancement similarly. Also, the public see no distinctions in gender especially in desire, trustworthiness and definitiveness. Women also have an advantage over men when it comes to honesty—one of the most crucial leadership traits, according to the public. While solid majorities of the public see no difference between men and women on decisiveness and ambition, among those who do draw a distinction on these traits, men have an edge over women. Some 27% of adults say that men are more decisive than women. By far most of general society (80%) says that men and women make similarly great business leaders, yet many feel organizations are not prepared to accept females for top leader positions. People concur that the two sexual gender are similarly fit for leading in the business world, and there is general settlement on this across ages and sectarian gatherings.

Up to this point, leadership roles have prevalently been held by men and men were hence generalized to be more successful leaders. Ladies were seldom found in senior administrative roles prompting an absence of information on how they act in such positions. However, momentum research has found an adjustment of pattern and ladies have become more predominant in the labor force throughout the course of recent many years, particularly in administration and leading roles. The orientation hole is diminishing and these generalizations are changing as additional ladies enter positions of authority. The information from the essential writing on this point to the two principal lines of exploration going against each other, the first being that there are little, yet by and by critical sex contrasts in administration and the second being that leading doesn't meaningfully affect authority. One theory goes that society generally associates successful leadership with stereotypically 'masculine' traits such as assertiveness and dominance, and so disapproves of female leaders because they violate these gender norms. With this women go through greater obstacles to reaching the upper chamber of leadership. In a study publish in the journal of Applied Psychology to add an insight to the gender leadership comparison by breaking down the aftereffects of 99 distinct examinations with deliberate leaders' viability from 1962 to 2011, the specialists were unable to pick the circumstances wherein male or female leaders succeeded.

In all studies, no gender is above the other.it all depends on the view of human and whosoever want to lead. Leadership does not condemn gender. Gender only bring diversity to leadership.

EFFECTIVE LEADERSHIP.

How about we cut to the chase: No fruitful association would have been where it is today without successful authority. Effective leadership is quite often one of the principal and essential drivers for development, improvement and advancement. Also, observe, leadership isn't about the titles, or even the awards. Effective Leadership is significantly more effective and significant. It is procured and worked for. There is no set recipe or bit by bit plan, it relies upon the way of life and necessities of the association. Effective Leadership sparkles while the going is great, yet additionally (significantly more in this way) when things are unpleasant. They're regarded (not dreaded) by individuals around them, who thus, become persuaded to work harder and make more huge commitments to the improvement of the association too.

Leadership isn't tied in with pursuing an objective without any assistance. As a matter of fact, Leadership is tied in with moving and spurring individuals to cooperate towards an objective. As an article from Pennsylvania State University states, "Effective Leadership is fundamental for a working society." In a more limited size, the reality stays valid in associations and organizations. It's essentially outside the realm of possibilities for an organization to proceed to develop and develop with the times without powerful leadership. Particularly during this time where computerized innovation is changing each part of how business is being finished and the way that clients are drawing in with brands. A brand without viable leaders will resemble a boat cruising without a commander guiding what direction to head.

FACTORS OF EFFECTIVE LEADERSHIP

SUCCESS.

Leadership is the achievement of an objective through the bearing of human cooperations. The one who effectively pushes his human partners to accomplish specific closures is a leader. An extraordinary leader is one who can do so a large number of days, and many years, in a wide assortment of conditions. He may not have or show power; force and the danger of damage might in all likelihood never go into his dealings. He may not be well known; his supporters might in all likelihood never do what he wishes out of adoration or profound respect for him. He may not at any point be a brilliant individual; he might very well never utilize important gadgets to perform his visions or to focus on his administration. With respect to the significant matter of putting forth objectives, he may really take care of business of little impact, or even of little expertise; as a leader he may simply complete the plans of others.

He for the most part doesn't concentrate on leadership by any means. Rather he concentrates on prevalence, power, dramatic artistry, or shrewdness in lengthy reach arranging. A few leaders have these things, yet they are not on the pitch of leadership. His unique achievement is a human and social one which stems from his understanding of his fellow workers and the relationship of their individual goals to the group goal that he must carry out.

PROBLEMS AND ILLUSIONS

It isn't difficult to state in a couple of words what successful leaders do that makes them effective. In any case, it is a lot harder to pick out the parts that decide their prosperity. The standard strategy is to give sufficient acknowledgment of every workers capability with the goal that he can predict the fulfillment of some significant interest or rationale of his, in the completing of the whole group endeavor. Rough types of leadership depend entirely on single wellsprings of fulfillment like financial prizes or the easing of fears about different sorts of weakness. People are not machines with a solitary arrangement of press buttons. At the point when their complex reactions to love, prestige, freedom, accomplishment, and group enrollment are unnoticed at work, they perform, best case scenario, as automata who bring not exactly their greatest proficiency to the task get been to them, and even from a pessimistic standpoint as insubordinate slaves who intentionally or unknowingly harm the exercises they should further.

It is ironic that our basic image of "the leader" is so often that of a military commander, because— at least—military organizations are the purest example of an unimaginative application of simple reward and punishment as motivating devices. We have all heard the cry, "someone must be the Boss," and I guess nobody would genuinely disagree. Be that as it may, it is hazardous to confound the levels of leadership or table of association with a technique for finishing things. It is rather similar to the diagram of a football play which shows a general arrangement and how every individual adds to it.

The chart isn't Leadership. Without anyone else, it has no bearing somehow on how the play will be. However that very question of successful execution is the issue of leadership. Prizes and punishments might assist every followers with doing his task, however over the long run assuming that achievement is to be proceeding and the morale is to be consistent, every follower should not just completely grasp his part and its connection to the collective endeavor; he should likewise WANT to do it. The issue of each and every leader is to create these WANTS and to track down ways of diverting existing WANTS into effective cooperation

RELATIONSHIP WITH OTHERS

At the point when the leader succeeds, it will be on the grounds that he has learned two fundamental examples: Men are different, and men are unique. Individuals answer not exclusively to the conventional ways utilized by the driver of a jackass but to desire, enthusiasm, love of the great and the delightful, fatigue, self-question, and a lot more aspects and examples of thought and feeling that make them men. Be that as it may, the strength and significance of these interests are not the same for every followe nor is how much they can be fulfilled in their work.

For example:
One man might be described essentially by a religious rule and however find out that it is in reality very immaterial to his day to day work.

One more might track down his fundamental fulfillments in tackling scholar issues and never find how his adoration for Chess and mathematical riddles can be applied to his business.

Or on the other hand, another may need a well disposed, respecting relationship that he wants at home and be continually baffled by the disappointment of his boss not to recognize and exploit that need. For followers to perceive their leader as he truly is might be as difficult as it could be for him to totally figure out them. A portion of the obvious challenges of connections among bosses and subordinates come from wrong perception. What we comprehend in our general surroundings is shaded by the originations and biases we start with. My view on my Leader or superior might be so hued by assumptions in the way of behaving of different leaders that may not show up similarly to him. Suppose that I show two groups of observers a film of an exchange of views between an employer and his subordinate. The scene portrays disagreement followed by anger and dismissal. The blame will be assigned very differently by the two groups if I have shown one, a scene of the worker earlier in a happy, loving family breakfast setting, while the other group has seen instead a breakfast-table scene where the worker snarls at his family and storms out of the house. The altercation will be understood altogether differently by people who have had favorable or unfavorable glimpses of the character in question.

An ideal association ought to have workers/followers at each level answering to someone whose domain is high enough to empower him to be aware of the people who report to him.

CONCLUSION

No choice merits the name except if it implies the adjusting of dangers and returns. If it be sure, we wouldn't require a man to utilize his judgment about it. Mistakes are inescapable. What we should expect of representatives is that they gain from their mistakes, not that they never make them. It ought to be the leader's anxiety to watch the drawn out development of his men to see that, as they learn, their triumphs progressively offset their disappointments.

This idea of long-run development is a crucial piece of proceeding with leadership. Each man should be allowed to realize that his job in the organization is dependent upon improvement and that its advancement is restricted exclusively by his commitments. Particularly, he should see the leader as the man generally intrigued by and supportive toward his development. It isn't sufficient to have intrigued work force officials or other staff individuals who assume no part in arrangement making. Notwithstanding all the help they can deliver in specialized ways, they can never replace an interest with respect to the dependable chief.

I hope this help to sharpen and give you a new perspective of becoming a leader. I know there are many more but in this book we look at main keys and if you really read this book, understand and implement it you are on the verge of being the REAL BOSS.

www.ingramcontent.com/pod-product-compliance
Lightning Source LLC
Chambersburg PA
CBHW030454220526
45464CB00006B/2539